AN ALBUM OF
ROCK AND ROLL

I'M BROKE
Frankie Avalon
Michael Jackson
Thriller
Grateful Dead
American Beauty
ELVIS COSTELLO
AND THE ATTRACTIONS
GOOD
LOVIN'
LIPSTICK ON YOUR COLLAR
FRANKIE
MGM
NEVER BE ANYONE ELSE BUT YOU
IT'S LATE
RICKY NELSON
SEARCHIN' · IDOL WITH THE GOLDEN HEAD
YOUNG BLOOD · MY BABY COMES TO ME
ATCO EP 4501

AN ALBUM OF

ROCK AND ROLL

TRUDY J. HANMER

FRANKLIN WATTS • 1988
NEW YORK • LONDON • TORONTO • SYDNEY

For Sally "Joe" Hanmer

Cover photograph courtesy of Comstock

Photographs courtesy of: Ginger Giles: p. 2; Michael Ochs Archives/
Venice, CA: pp. 10 (top), 13 (all three), 20, 25 (right), 29, 33, 36, 38
(both), 39, 41, 47 (bottom); Frank Driggs Collection: pp. 11, 22, 28, 50 (middle
left), 57 (left), 58 (bottom), 60 (top), 77 (all), 83, 84; UPI/Bettmann
Newsphotos: pp. 10 (bottom), 18, 25 (left), 44, 58 (top); The New York
Public Library at Lincoln Center: pp. 27 (top: Warner Bros. Records),
42, 47 (top), 50 (middle right and bottom), 57 (right top and bottom), 60
(bottom), 64 (both), 72 (both); AP/Wide World Photos: pp. 27 (bottom), 34
(both), 50 (top), 52, 63 (top), 81 (bottom), 91 (top), 92 (top); Ren Grevatt
Associates: p. 63 (bottom); Warner/Reprise: p. 69; Sire Records Company:
pp. 71 (top), 81 (top left); ARISTA Records: p. 71 (bottom);
Island Records: p. 74; Sarah McMullen & Company: p. 76 (© Bob Alford);
Sheila Escovedo: p. 80 (top); Annie Leibovitz: p. 80 (left); LGI: pp. 80
(right: Nick Elgar), 87 (top: Lynn Goldsmith); MTV: p. 87 (bottom);
Showtime: p. 88 (left); Paul McAlpine: p. 88 (top); Jean Pagliuso: p. 89;
Retna: p. 91 (bottom); Henry Diltz: p. 92 (bottom).

Library of Congress Cataloging-in-Publication Data

Hanmer, Trudy J.
An album of rock and roll.

Includes index.
Summary: Traces the history of rock and roll music
from its roots in blues and gospel to the present day
and discusses its themes, changing styles, hits, and
leading personalities.
1. Rock music—History and criticism—Juvenile
literature. [1. Rock music—History and criticism]
I. Title.
ML3534.H35 1988   784.5′4′009   86-28110
ISBN 0-531-10318-8

CONTENTS

CHAPTER ONE

THE BEGINNINGS

THE ENDURING
LEGACY OF
BLACK MUSIC

Prince. Dylan. The Boss. The Beatles. Chuck Berry. The Top Forty. Madonna. Wolfman Jack. Whitney Houston. Bo Diddley. The Top Ten. Michael Jackson. The Platters. Elvis Presley. The Shirelles. Boz Scaggs. Diana Ross. Ricky Nelson. Rock. Hard rock. Soft rock. Heavy metal. Bubble gum.

Performers, phrases, musical styles—what is the musical phenomenon that includes them all? What is the sound that has endured for three generations, the sound that has dominated popular music for more than three decades? It's the sound of rock and roll!

But what exactly is rock and roll? Where did it come from? Who invented it? Is there really a connection between Buddy Holly and Prince, between Janis Joplin and Madonna, between the Four Freshmen and the Grateful Dead?

People have many different definitions for rock and roll. Most rock and roll fans agree on two things, however: first, that rock and roll is a predominantly American music form and second, that rock and roll has commanded the national and international music scene since the early 1950s.

In 1922 a black woman blues singer, Trixie Smith, sang ''My Daddy Rocks Me (With One Steady Roll),'' probably the first number to link "rock" and "roll" in its title. In 1931 Duke Ellington recorded "Rockin' in Rhythm," and throughout the thirties and forties a variety of singers made a handful of records using the term. What all these artists had in common was their race. They were all black musicians; and, at that time in American history, they played almost exclusively for black audiences.

Modern rock and roll musicians acknowledge the large debt that American rock music owes to early black musicians. Rock and roll is not exclusively the child of black music, but without black music, rock and roll might never have been born. To understand the influence of black music on rock and roll, it is necessary to understand the climate of racism and oppression in which American black musicians worked for centuries.

Until after World War II music in the United States was as segregated as all other aspects of social life between the two races. In many ways the end of slavery had widened this separation. In post–Civil War America white and black people began to develop parallel lives. There were segregated schools, segregated churches, segregated neighborhoods, segregated businesses and segregated means of transportation. Among other things, black people were relegated to separate bathrooms and drinking fountains and separate seats in movie theaters. They were denied access to restaurants, hotels, voting, and jury duty. There were white theaters and black theaters, white night clubs and black night clubs, white music and black music.

Music had long been a significant force in the lives of black people, slave and free. And, in spite of segregation, white people had long copied black music and claimed the best of it for their own. Even before the Civil War white musicians along Tin Pan Alley (the traditional Manhattan home of the songwriting business) "borrowed" tunes and lyrics from black slave musicians who had no access to the music business. In the nineteenth century the music business revolved around the publication of sheet music for pianos, and songwriters were always searching for new material. One early nineteenth-century white musician wrote, "Let one [Negro] in the swamps of Carolina compose a new song, and it is written down, amended (that is, almost spoilt), printed. . . . Meanwhile, the poor author digs away with his hoe, utterly ignorant of his greatness."

What was true in the nineteenth century was still true in the 1940s and 1950s. And throughout most of the 1950s there were distinct music charts: "Rhythm and Blues" for black songs by black artists and "Pop" (for "popular") and "Country and Western" for white artists. In 1949, just prior to the recording of the first rock and roll hits, *Billboard*, the leading publication of the music industry, changed the title of its black record chart from "race" to "rhythm and blues." But major recording companies in the fifties continued to use the word "race" as a designation for those few black singers under contract to the big recording companies. Among such performers in the thirties, forties, and fifties were "middle-of-the-road" crooners like Nat "King" Cole and the Mills Brothers. They sang soft, well-harmonized songs that were not really reflective of what was happening in the black music world. Although theirs was a legitimate black sound, it was a safe sound, acceptable to the large recording companies.

What was happening in the black music world was about to cross into the white music world to create rock and roll. Black musicians throughout the twentieth century had been renowned for two kinds of music often copied by white musicians—jazz and blues. Jazz, with its home in New Orleans, was urban black music. Jazz used horns and unusual syncopated rhythms and depended on the improvisations of the band members for its greatness.

The "blues" was the music of rural areas. Blues were songs that repeated a single line several times and were originally known as "one verse songs." Perhaps more than any other song type, the blues brought black female singers to prominence, from Gertrude "Ma" Rainey of vaudeville fame to Billie Holiday and Bessie Smith. By the late 1930s both blues and jazz were using a relatively new instrument: the electric guitar. A black guitarist, Aaron "T-Bone" Walker, is credited with playing this instrument in a way that would lead to the rock guitar music of artists as diverse as Chuck Berry, Jimi Hendrix, and the Beatles.

The electric guitar, plus the migration of thousands of black people to urban industrial centers during World War II, led to cross-overs between jazz and the blues. This new music, often called "jump blues," featured a fast rhythm, an electric lead guitar, and a saxophone. Jump blues songs in the late 1940s were very close to

Left: *Bessie Smith, the widely influential blues singer.* Facing page: *A 1930s Dixieland jazz band. Jazz is based on a strong and syncopated beat— the same foundation as rock and roll.*

Right: *Singer Billie Holiday's vocal style incorporated blues with jazz.*

the rock and roll sound that would dominate the next decade. For example, the hit tune "K.C. Loving," by Little Willie Littlefield, would become the rock and roll classic "Kansas City." Another jump blues number, "Good Rockin' Tonight," recorded in 1947 by Roy Brown, has been called by *Rolling Stone* "the most seminal of all jump blues hits."

Besides jazz and blues, a third aspect of black music greatly influenced the development of rock and roll. This was gospel or church music. Music had been central to African tribal spiritualism and remained dominant in the services of southern black Christians. Many black singers, from Nat "King" Cole to Little Richard (and a number of white southern singers, including Elvis Presley), began their public singing careers in their families' churches. These performers used the gospel sound, but added to it lyrics about love and romance, which were definitely nongospel. "Rhythm and gospel" became a separate record category that defined songs like those recorded by the Dominoes and the Drifters in the immediate prerock era.

Gospel contributed some distinct vocal characteristics to popular music: melismas and question-and-answer lyrics. Melismas are series of notes that a lead vocalist—first in a choir and later in a singing group—uses to fit a single syllable of lyrics. These notes were frequently improvised by the lead singer, which means that they had not been included in the music by the songwriter and were rarely sung in the same way twice. Question-and-answer—or "call-and-response"—lyrics traced their beginnings to early black churches where the congregation was too poor to have enough hymnals for everyone. Consequently the minister or choir would sing the verses and the members of the church congregation would sing back the chorus in response.

Black church music was also characterized by its use of such instruments as the guitar, drums, or horns. Because of the poverty of most black congregations, pianos and organs were financially impossible. By making do with those musical instruments that they could afford, black churches instilled in their young parishioners a feeling for rhythm guitars and drums that would carry over into recordings of popular music. The Clovers, the Midnighters, Etta James, and Jackie Wilson, all early rock stars, were gospel and rhythm singers first.

Jump-blues musician Little Willie Littlefield. Like rock and roll, jump blues had a good beat, and you could dance to it.

The Platters (right) and the Flamingos (left), two rhythm and blues groups who adapted gospel harmonizing to sentimental pop music

When gospel, jazz, and rhythm and blues mixed with the white country sound in the early 1950s, rock and roll began. In the beginning it looked as though black rock and roll music would suffer the same fate as earlier types of black music. The 1954 hit in Los Angeles, "Sh-Boom," by the black group the Chords, did not become a smash on a national level until it was recorded by an all-white group, the Crew-Cuts.

"Covering," rerecording a song first recorded by someone else, became standard white practice in the early fifties. White musicians looking for new material "covered" a multitude of black songs. Perry Como took "Kokomo" from Gene and Eunice, the McGuire Sisters took "Sincerely" from the Moonglows, Teresa Brewer took "A Tear Fell" from Ivory Joe Hunter, and Pat Boone covered several songs first recorded by such black artists as Fats Domino and the Flamingos. With the music industry strictly segregated and all the big national companies controlled by white people, it was still impossible for black musicians to make a name for themselves nationally—unless they were willing to sing middle-of-the-road tunes. National companies believed that black music had to be cleaned up or "whitewashed" by white groups before it would sell to the majority white audience.

In 1955 nine songs made it to the number one position on the Rhythm and Blues charts. Two songs by the Platters, "Only You" and "The Great Pretender," were among these. A year later, in 1956, two more Platters numbers made the top of the charts, but this time they were on the Pop charts. At the same time, a new young white singing sensation, Elvis Presley, was number one on both the Pop and the Rhythm and Blues charts. After 1956 the music charts would be integrated. Rhythm and blues would no longer be a euphemism for black.

The integration of white and black musicians took place during a very important decade in black history. Almost simultaneously with the crossover of the Platters from rhythm and blues to pop came the 1954 United States Supreme Court decision *Brown vs. Board of Education.* In this famous court case, the Supreme Court ruled that segregation was not "separate and equal," a position long held by white people. Separate facilities for black people, said the court, were too often unequal and, in fact, inferior. This was the first step in the long road toward full integration of black Americans into American society.

The *Brown* decision helped hasten the acceptance among musicians of black artists on the popular charts. Unfortunately, a second result was an immediate backlash of racism. The new rock and roll music was attacked as a symptom of the evils that would come with integration. Rock and roll music was fast, wild, young, and frequently accompanied by wild dancing. Many in the older generation were nervous about the impact of rock and roll on teenagers. Racists among the older generation claimed rock and roll's black connection was the source of all misdoing by teenagers.

Few black musicians were immune from attack. In one of the most widely publicized incidents of the period, Nat "King" Cole was dragged from the stage during a concert in Birmingham, Alabama, in 1956. Cole was not even a rock and roll singer, but his attackers, the White Citizens' Council, claimed that he and other black singers were part of a plot to ruin America. Although most Americans were shocked by this attack, it is also true that the Nat "King" Cole television show left the air in 1956 because no sponsor could be found for a show as controversial as one starring a black man.

As the decade wore on and out, the civil rights movement of the 1960s brought new forms of integration and unprecedented success for the black musicians whose tempos and rhythm had given birth to rock and roll. The music industry continued to be dominated by white producers and white artists, however. John Lennon bragged in the 1960s, "We [the Beatles] sing more colored than the Africans." As late as the mid-seventies, the Scottish-born singer Rod Stewart explained to a reporter, "There are a lot of colored guys who can sing us off the stage, but half the battle is selling it, not singing it. It's the image, not what you sing."

Many young white rock and roll singers have tried to pay their debts to their black predecessors. Janis Joplin bought a tombstone for her heroine, Bessie Smith. Pete Townshend wrote a song for his group, the Who, in which he acknowledged the legions of black singers who had paved the way for modern rock singers like himself. Wrote Townshend, "I look all white, but my dad was black."

In spite of these efforts, many great black artists died without the national recognition they deserved, their songs known only to their loyal black fans because they were unable to gain access to white recording companies and white audiences. Some black musicians managed to find commercial success by leaving the United States. Jimi Hendrix, for example, was earning thirty dollars a week when he left the United States in 1966 to find fame and fortune in Great Britain. (Hendrix, his reputation made, returned to tour the United States a few years later at thirty thousand dollars a performance.) Other performers were not so lucky as Jimi Hendrix. Jesse Stone, Ella Mae Morse, the Trenier twins, Cecil Grant, and Louis Jordan never saw financial success to match their talents.

Rock and roll, the most lucrative entertainment medium in the world today, owes a great debt to these black musicians. They contributed jazz, blues, boogie-woogie, soul, jump blues, and gospel. They helped change the standards of songwriting. (Instead of a melody line thirty-two bars long, their songs used a repeated melody that was eight bars in length.) Black musicians showed how the guitar could be the lead instrument in a band, and they demonstrated the power of a simple, driving drum beat. Their vocals changed the way popular music was sung, and they added a new vocabulary to song lyrics from the black American experience.

One of the greats of black music and of early rock and roll, Chuck Berry, summarized the beginnings of rock and roll this way: "This rock bit, it's called rock now, but it used to be called boogie-woogie, it used to be blues, used to be called rhythm and blues, and it even went through a stage of what is known as funk. . . . Names of it can vary, but music that is inspiring to the head and heart, to dance by and cause you to tap your foot, it's there."

Whether the roots of rock are traced to African ring dances, to New Orleans blues and jazz, or to rural church choirs, the power of black music and the importance of the black contribution are central to the birth of rock and roll. The history of rock and roll is tied to American history. For years, segregated blacks made their own music outside the mainstream of American culture. In time this music would become the mainstream as the social barriers between the races began to topple and white teenagers adopted black music for their own.

CHAPTER TWO

ELVIS PRESLEY AND THE ROCKABILLY YEARS

ROCK AND ROLL DOMINATES THE NATIONAL CHARTS

In 1947 record sales in the United States topped $224 million. Ten years later record sales hit $460 million. In Great Britain during these same years the record industry nearly doubled its production. In both countries rock and roll records accounted for the increase. In the mid-1950s rock and roll exploded as young white singers began to popularize black tunes and to create their own rock and roll music.

Just as black music made great contributions to rock and roll, white country and western music was part of the new phenomenon as well. White male country and western artists were the first to borrow the repertories and techniques of black artists. Because of their isolation, rural white and black musicians came into frequent contact with each other. Although segregation was certainly the rule in small southern towns, black roadhouses held "white" nights when white people could come to hear black artists. In these small clubs barriers began to break down as black and white musicians jammed with each other. Socially taboo integration added an edge to music that was already exciting.

Bill Haley and His Comets were one of the first and certainly one of the most important of the little-known country and western groups to make it to national fame. During a nostalgia tour in 1969, Bill Haley told reporters, "Our music had to have affected all those people [the rock groups that came after] because we built the whole thing." Ha-

ley's analysis of his group's importance is a bit exaggerated. Nevertheless, the birth of rock and roll is often pinpointed at the 1954 recording of "Rock Around the Clock." This Bill Haley hit remains the all-time best-selling rock and roll single.

Bill Haley had started out as a conventional country and western singer. In the early years his group was called the Saddlemen. The members of the group all wore ten-gallon hats. In 1951 the Saddlemen had their first significant hit when they covered Jackie Brenston's "Rocket 88," a rock song about a car. They followed this up with "Rock the Joint" in 1952. Next came a name change for the group, the recording of "Rock Around the Clock," and instant—and enduring—stardom. "Rock Around the Clock" formed part of the soundtrack for the hit movie *Blackboard Jungle* (1955), a classic film about teenage rebellion.

Not all country and western groups moved as swiftly to stardom as Bill Haley's did. To get from small, out-of-the-way clubs in the rural South to a spot on the national charts was difficult. Blacks faced discrimination because of their color and whites because of the rawness of their new, unpolished sounds. To be "discovered," both groups—black and white—needed promoters. In 1951 such a man was found in the person of Alan Freed, a disc jockey from Cleveland, Ohio.

Freed gave prime air time to songs on the rhythm and blues charts, an unprecedented action for a white radio station. He soon had a devoted teenage following, white and black. In 1952 he capitalized on his growing audience by planning a huge, integrated rock and roll concert in Cleveland. Although eighty thousand tickets were sold, the show was cancelled by the city because the white citizens were uncomfortable with the prospect of an integrated audience.

Nevertheless, Freed—and rock and roll—were on their way. By 1954 Freed was a deejay for station WINS in New York City and was one of the most widely influential deejays in terms of getting new songs on the charts. Freed and other deejays like him, for example

Bill Haley and His Comets.
Fans thought the plump, balding
Haley (center) was a rebel.

Alan Freed's career as an innovative disc jockey was cut short by a payola scandal. He was accused of taking cash from record companies in exchange for playing their records.

Bob "Wolfman Jack" Smith, were the first to announce records in the Top Forty AM format. They gave air time to black artists and country rock groups whose records were not played on more traditional stations. The colorful personalities and distinctive styles of the most well-known deejays added to their appeal. One of Wolfman Jack's trademarks was his frequent practice of howling at the moon between songs.

In rock and roll's quest for national recognition, producer Sam Phillips was as important as the deejays. During the late forties and early fifties Phillips operated a small recording studio in Memphis, Tennessee, where he recorded black artists who had no other access to recording studios. In the beginning Phillips sold these records to bigger studios on the West Coast, but around 1952 he started his own Sun label. His secretary remembers Sam Phillips saying, "If I could find a white man who had the Negro sound and the Negro feel, I could make a billion dollars."

Sam Phillips found his singer in a man whose fame would far outshadow Bill Haley's success—Elvis Presley. Presley, like Haley, came from the musical tradition of white country and western—also known as hillbilly—music. Like no other singer before or since, Elvis would combine rock and hillbilly, called rockabilly, and make a lasting place for himself in American popular music.

Elvis was born in East Tupelo, Mississippi, on January 8, 1935. He was a twin whose brother, Jesse, died at birth. Elvis's parents, Vernon and Gladys Presley, never had much money, but what they had, they devoted to their only child. He, in turn, was devoted to them. His was a poor white, rural upbringing, complete with gospel singing in his family church and at state fairs. In later years Elvis recalled his early years at the Pentecostal First Assembly of God as the strongest musical influence in his life. When he was ten years old he won his first prize for public singing when he took fifth place for a country and western ballad that he crooned at the Mississippi-Alabama Fair and Dairy Show. At the age of eleven he got his first guitar.

In 1948 Elvis and his parents moved to Memphis, Tennessee. Here, Elvis, for the first time opposing his parents' wishes, associated with black rhythm and blues musicians. He was something of a loner at Humes High School where he graduated in 1953. Like his father he worked as a truck driver after graduation, but he kept visiting black clubs in the area.

In 1954 Elvis cut his first C&W chart hit, an old blues number titled "That's All Right," on Sam Phillips's Sun label. He was voted the eighth most promising new hillbilly artist that year. Then, in 1955, he made the national charts with another country and western number, "Baby, Let's Play House." Elvis's big break, however, came with the release of "Heartbreak Hotel" in January 1956. Elvis recorded hit after hit from 1956 until his induction into the army in 1958 brought a brief hiatus to his career. Fourteen of these hits, including "Jailhouse Rock," "Hound Dog," "Don't Be Cruel," "All Shook Up," and "Love Me Tender," were million sellers. For mid-1950s America, Elvis Presley defined rock and roll.

In an interview with a reporter from the *Saturday Evening Post* in 1956, Elvis chalked up his instant success to good luck. "I just fell into it, really," he was reported as saying. But there was more to Elvis's stardom than good luck. He and the other white country musicians who made the transition to rock in the 1950s were part of a revolutionary phase of American popular music. Added to Elvis's luck—the luck of being in the right place at the right time that plays a part in any great success story—were his ambition, his musical talent, and his sense of what the new teenage audience craved.

Presley's performances started riots. When he first appeared on TV's "Ed Sullivan Show," Elvis the Pelvis was filmed from the waist up.

Elvis has been compared to his contemporaries, the movie stars James Dean and Marlon Brando. What Elvis and other rockabilly stars had in common with these actors was their air of rebellion. All were young and all seemed to sneer in the face of establishment and tradition. Rock music itself, with its pounding rhythms and wild dancing, was unsettling to the older generation. Elvis embodied this threat—his music was sexy, wild, and untamed. Furthermore, he looked tough, surly, and unmanageable. Country singer Bob Luman reminisced about seeing Elvis at an early concert: "This cat came out in red pants and a green coat and a pink shirt and socks, and he had this sneer on his face . . ."

It was a sneer that thrilled millions of teenagers who found in Elvis a hero for their generation. The United States in the 1950s seemed slow, dull, and complacent to many young people. Dwight Eisenhower, the oldest man ever to hold the office, was president, and World War II veterans were busy building a new life in suburbia with their families. Teenagers as a group, with their own tastes, idols, and interests, began to assume their own identity, very much apart from their elders. Elvis was one force around which they united.

The early years of rock and roll spawned a teenage culture. When Elvis stood on the platform of the concert stage, he was saying to teenagers, "See, I can make music that sells, I can be successful, I can be a star, too." Elvis's very presence as a star was a slap in the face to proponents of traditional paths to wealth and fame. However, Elvis was no rebel against the American way of life. He did nothing to reject material success as it had long been defined in America. He bought clothes, cars, a mansion. To the increasingly consumer-conscious teenagers he represented "making it" in the face of overwhelming odds. Furthermore, he made it on his own youthful terms.

Rockabilly has been characterized by *Rolling Stone* as the "purest of all rock and roll genres." It lasted roughly from 1956 to 1958. During those few years, musicians like Presley, Carl Perkins, Jerry Lee Lewis, Gene Vincent, and Eddie Cochran dominated the popular music scene. Perkins, in fact, was the first to hit the number one spot on the Pop and Rhythm and Blues charts simultaneously. He did this with his recording of "Blue Suede Shoes" in 1956. By 1958 the rockabillies' heyday had ended. Presley was in the army, Lewis had been banned from the airwaves for a controversial marriage, and Perkins, with rockabilly on the wane, switched to pure country. While on tour together in England in 1960, Cochran was killed and Vincent seriously injured in an automobile accident.

In their prime, though, rockabilly stars produced music that was notable for its beat, its lyrics, and its vocal technique. The beat was up-tempo, the accent was off-tempo, and the lead guitar was often accompanied by a slapping bass, a holdover from the country and western sound. The lyrics were often nonsense syllables that borrowed heavily from the "doo-wop" harmonizing of black groups such as the Platters and the Coasters. The singers vocalized strings of syllables over the background guitars. The vocals on rockabilly songs also featured hiccups, stutters, and vibrato warbling by the lead singers. Many records featured echoes by backup groups that sounded a lot like the gospel call-and-response choruses.

Jerry Lee Lewis was typical of this group. Born in Ferriday, Louisiana, in 1935, Lewis had his first big national hit in 1956 with "A Whole Lotta Shakin' Goin' On." This was followed in 1957 by his biggest hit, "Great Balls of Fire." In 1958 Lewis passed from the music scene when he married his thirteen-year-old cousin. What was acceptable in rural backwoods Louisiana was not acceptable to the management of large record companies who were trying to sell records to teenagers whose conservative, middle-class parents frequently controlled their allowances.

Buddy Holly was a contemporary of the rockabilly stars, but one who charted his own course in a distinctive way. Holly was born on September 7, 1936, and died in an airplane crash on February 3, 1959, while touring with fellow stars Ritchie Valens and the Big Bopper, who also lost their lives in the crash. In his brief career Holly had seven Top Forty hits.

Buddy Holly was a gawky figure who wore glasses and a dark suit on stage. He and his group, the Crickets, were young, and they sang of young love. Holly's hit song "Peggy Sue" introduced one of the first rock and roll music heroines. Like Presley, Lewis, and others, Holly had a voice that ranged from falsetto to bass. His songs were filled with nursery-rhyme lyrics. More important than his few hit records was the fact that Holly was a talented songwriter who performed his own music. His recordings demonstrated a number of

Left: *Jerry Lee Lewis—a whole lot of jumpin' goin' on.*
Right: *Buddy Holly's recording career lasted only a year and a half—long enough to change the future of rock and roll.*

innovations that would be imitated by other groups. He and the Crickets were the first white group to feature two guitars (lead and rhythm), a bass, and drums as their standard instruments. Holly was also the first to double-track his voice and guitar, and he was the first to use a string accompaniment on a rock and roll record.

Few people agree on the meaning of all the symbolism in Don McLean's 1971 hit, "American Pie," but most would acknowledge that the day the plane carrying Holly, Valens, and the Big Bopper crashed was "the day the music died." McLean himself told *Life* magazine in 1972, "Buddy Holly was the first and last person I ever idolized as a kid."

One popular white duo of the mid-fifties is still making music today. Never as titanic as Elvis or Buddy Holly, the Everly Brothers, Don and Phil, made the transition from country and western to pop with their release of "Bye Bye Love" in 1957. The Everly Brothers sang about teenagers in love and the pressures they faced from parents, friends, and school. They sang in extremely close harmony, with only a third of a note difference between their voices. This close pairing of voices was typical of white country harmony.

At the same time that the white rockabilly stars Buddy Holly and the Everly Brothers were hitting their stride, black artists, freed from their exclusive position on the Rhythm and Blues charts, made important rock and roll recordings. Among them was Fats Domino. Born Antoine Domino in 1928, Fats was nearly a decade older than most of the young white rockers. He had been singing rock and roll for a long time before it officially had a name, and he would continue singing long after the fifties died out. By 1980 Domino had sold sixty-five million records. He had more gold hits to his name than any other artist except Elvis and the Beatles.

In 1955 Fats broke out of the "race charts" with "Ain't That a Shame." In all of Fats Domino's songs there were echoes of his childhood among the jazz musicians of New Orleans. Fats's sound was smooth; the piano was the most important instrument backing him up and reflected the boogie-woogie music of Bourbon Street. His biggest hit was "Blueberry Hill," recorded in 1956.

Another black Southerner who hit the top of the charts in the 1950s was Little Richard. Born in Macon, Georgia, in 1935, Richard Penniman was one of a large family (twelve or thirteen children—

Above: *Phil (left) and Don Everly's cheerful recording, "Wake Up Little Susie" was banned from some radio stations. The heroine of the song falls asleep on a date and spends the night with her boyfriend. Below: Fats "the Fat Man" Domino*

"A-wop-lop-a-loo-bop-a-wop-bam-boom," sang Little Richard.

accounts differ). When he was thrown out of his house as a young teenager, Little Richard went to live with people who owned a nightclub where he soon began performing. By the time he turned sixteen he had signed a record contract. In 1955 his recording of "Tutti-Frutti" exploded on the music world. Little Richard's music, more than that of any other popular black singer of the mid-fifties, thrilled and threatened white audiences with its power, sensuality, and brashness. His shouting vocals and wild style characterized such hits as "Long Tall Sally" and "Good Golly, Miss Molly." Little Richard gave up rock music at the beginning of the 1960s, but his early hits were central to the birth of rock and roll in the 1950s.

Chuck Berry
demonstrating
his trademark
"duck walk"

In September 1955 Chuck Berry crossed over from the Rhythm and Blues to the Pop charts with "Maybellene." Berry has been called the "greatest rock and roller" and "the greatest rock lyricist this side of Bob Dylan." Like Little Richard, Chuck Berry was born into a lower-middle-class southern black family. Before becoming a star he had worked as a beautician. (He learned this trade in a reform school where he was sent because of a robbery conviction.) At the height of his career in 1959, Berry was sentenced to prison. Many people believed that the charges against Berry were trumped up. Nevertheless, he served two years in prison. He would go to prison again in the 1970s for income tax evasion. His brushes with the law, however, did not stop him from creating wonderful music.

What Berry was able to do better than any other rock guitarist of his time was combine the blues with country and western guitar playing to create a style all his own—a style that came to mean rock music. Whether his lyrics were greater than those of Dylan or not, the best of them evoked the life of the 1950s teenager. "School Day," his 1957 hit, chronicled the anguish of waiting for the bell to end the boredom of the classroom. "Sweet Little Sixteen" (1958) and "Johnny B. Goode" (1958) were other Berry hits with adolescent themes.

The 1950s are often described as the decade of conformity. Historians of the Eisenhower years lament the banality of the period, the sameness and the staleness. Yet this same decade saw the birth of one of the most powerful musical phenomena in western history. Out of the tensions of a generation gap (produced in part, at least, by the conformist, don't-rock-the-boat attitudes of the older generation) grew rock and roll. The cast included white musicians representing rebellious youth and black musicians who foreshadowed the long-overdue upheaval in the nation's race relations. Neither group wanted to overthrow American society; both groups wanted their fair share. In grasping for their pieces of the pie, they moved their music from small clubs and roadhouses to the mainstream Top 40 on the AM dial.

CHAPTER THREE

MASS PRODUCTION OF ROCK AND ROLL

TEEN STARS, GIRL GROUPS, AND MOTOWN

To the older generation, Elvis Presley and his contemporaries may have been a sign that the nation was headed to rack and ruin. To teenagers, Elvis and other rockers were a sign that music could be young, exciting, and annoying to their parents. To record companies, however, the signs that were important were dollar signs. By 1958 the music industry was convinced that rock and roll was a marketable commodity. Baby boomers—children born in the immediate post–World War II era—were growing into teenagers. They had money to spend and they spent it on rock and roll. The rock and roll consumers might be too young to vote, but they were old enough to buy. Not only did they purchase records in unprecedented quantities, but they also bought posters, bubble gum, candy, magazines, clothes, and any other paraphernalia connected with their favorite stars.

After 1958, record companies began to create new stars who could sell rock and roll music. Between 1958 and 1964 teenage singing stars took over the rock and roll world. The new stars were clean and wholesome. They sang rock and roll songs, but they did not present the image of rebellion that the rockabilly stars had.

The new singers gave rock and roll respectability in the eyes of the older generation. Unlike their predecessors, they did not usually write their own music, and the songs were often characterized by mass-produced lyrics. To adults the music was still too loud, the lyrics were still foolish, but the artists were clean-cut, and the songs' chief concerns were those of high school romance. The raunchy sexiness of the rhythm and blues numbers from the early 1950s was erased.

Record companies at this time hired teams of songwriters to produce hits for the singers they had under contract. Among the more prolific of these were Jerry Lieber and Mike Stoller, each of whom was earning $75,000 a year in 1958 when *Time* magazine dubbed them "kings of the state of annoyance known as rock and roll." Lieber and Stoller wrote such hits as "Yakety Yak" and "Charlie Brown" for the Coasters in 1958 and 1959. Their songs centered on the world of the 1950s teenager where dating and dances were the premier pastimes, automobiles vied with girls for boys' attention, and parents and high school were the only sources of pain.

In April 1959 *Time* quoted Jerry Lieber as saying, "Kids nine to fourteen make up our market and this is the stuff they want to hear." In a very brief period of time rock and roll music had stopped being an exciting, dangerous new force in the music world. The music had become the property of teenagers willing to listen to the same musical formulae with slightly altered lyrics. Sock hops and dancing were in, and the new artists provided countless dance tunes.

Lieber and Stoller were only two of the songwriters cranking out the hits. Many people believed that the best music came from the Brill Building on Broadway in New York City. Here teams of songwriters, including peole like Carole King and Neil Sedaka, who would later become performers, churned out song after song aimed at the new teenage audience. Besides King and Sedaka, the Brill Building boasted such writers as Cynthia Weil, Barry Mann, Gerry Goffin, and Howard Greenfield. They would create a song which would then be sold to a major recording studio, such as Columbia or RCA, as a

In the offices of the Brill Building in New York City, songwriters like Cynthia Weil (standing, left), Carole King, and Barry Mann supplied a steady stream of pop tunes for the day's teen idols.

Dick Clark (upper left), host of "American Bandstand," played disc jockey and chaperone to America's teenagers. The program showcased new dance crazes like the Twist (right).

vehicle for one of the stars under contract there. Through this process, hits like "Calendar Girl" (Neil Sedaka, 1961), "A Teenager in Love" (Dion and the Belmonts, 1959), and "Walking in the Rain" (Ronettes, 1964) made it to the charts.

Television played a major role in establishing the new teen stars. Of greatest importance was "American Bandstand." Hosted by Dick Clark and televised from Philadelphia, "American Bandstand" served as a showcase for new songs and new stars. In addition to "American Bandstand," television shows, both comic and dramatic, often produced singing stars. The "Mickey Mouse Club" had Annette Funicello; "The Donna Reed Show" had Shelly Fabares and Paul Petersen, the television brother and sister team; and "Ozzie and Harriet" (Ozzie a former Big Band conductor, Harriet his lead singer) produced—both on the screen and in real life—Ricky Nelson.

For a while it seemed as though any young television star could be a rock and roll star, too. A prime example of this phenomenon was Ed Byrnes, a young actor who played Kookie on the detective series "77 Sunset Strip." Kookie was a parking lot attendant with a mania for combing his hair. In the spring of 1959 Byrnes joined with Connie Stevens, another combination singing and television star, to record "Kookie, Kookie (Lend Me Your Comb)," a popular hit *Time* magazine praised as "a wolfish ditty."

Silly lyrics about nonsense subjects characterized many of the rock and roll hits of the late fifties and early sixties. Top numbers in 1958 included "Purple People Eater" by Sheb Wooley, "Short Shorts" by the Royal Teens, "Witch Doctor" by David Seville, "Lollipop" by the Chordettes, and "Splish Splash" by Bobby Darin. (It was also the year in which singing chipmunks, along with their human helper, David Seville of "Witch Doctor" fame, made it to the top of the charts.) In 1959 "Pink Shoelaces" by Dodie Stevens, and in 1960 "Itsy Bitsy Teenie Weenie Yellow Polka Dot Bikini" by Brian Hyland made it to the number two position on the Top Ten. Other unusual song topics became equally unusual dance steps: "Mashed Potato Time" (Dee Dee Sharp, 1962), "The Loco-Motion" (Little Eva, 1962), "The Monkey Time" (Major Lance, 1963), "Monster Mash" (Bobby "Boris" Pickett and the Crypt Kickers, 1962), and perhaps the biggest of all, Chubby Checker's "The Twist" (1960).

*Dick Clark (second from left) interviews a few teen idols
and dreamboats: Fabian (partially hidden), Neil Sedaka,
Freddy Cannon, Bobby Rydell, and Chubby Checker.*

Most of the biggest hits of these years were recorded by hand-
some young male singers, including Ricky Nelson, Bobby Darin, Paul
Anka, Fabian, Bobby Rydell, and Frankie Avalon. The titles of their
hits are a true index of the concerns of the teenage world at the end
of the 1950s—at least the concerns of the teenage world as they
were interpreted by the music industry. Ricky Nelson sang "Stood
Up" (1958), "Poor Little Fool" (1958), and "It's Late" (1959), about
the trials and tribulations of teenage dating. Bobby Darin contributed
"Queen of the Hop" (1958) and "Dream Lover" (1959) to the growing repertory of songs about young love. Paul Anka added to the
picture with "Diana" (1957), "Lonely Boy" (1959), and "Puppy
Love" (1960), three of his eight Top Ten singles between 1957 and
1961. Bobby Rydell chimed in with "Swingin' School" (1960) and
"Forget Him" (1964), while Frankie Avalon sang of "Venus" (1959),
"A Boy without a Girl" (1959), and that wonderful time "(When a Girl
Changes from) Bobby Sox to Stockings" (1959).

Of the top fifty singles on the popular rock and roll charts in 1958, only two were solo women vocals; at no point between 1958 and 1964 were even 10 percent of the top singles hits by solo women artists. The rock and roll that was being manufactured according to the "American Bandstand" formula featured male heroes who sang of women as objects of love, longing, and dreams.

If single vocals by females were rare, group singing by females was not. The early sixties was the era of a rock and roll phenomenon known as "girl groups." In 1960 the Shirelles first hit the Top Ten with "Will You Love Me Tomorrow." Between 1961 and 1963 the Shirelles had six more Top Ten singles, including "Dedicated to the One I Love," "Mama Said," and "Soldier Boy."

Girl groups were composed of young female singers, three or four to a group, usually black, and usually under contract to white male producers who provided them with their music. The singers in girl groups wore bouffant hairstyles, sequined, glittery outfits, and even when the members of the group were not related, they dressed identically and looked like sisters. In an era when roles for girls were strictly outlined, the girl groups often sang of their love for boys who were out-of-bounds, boys who were rebels, boys who came from "the wrong side of town." It was one way to strike a blow for freedom in a highly sexist culture.

The girl groups sang the tunes that Carole King, Gerry Goffin, Jeff Barry, Ellie Greenwich, Barry Mann, and Cynthia Weil were writing in the Brill Building. They also sang music written by Phil Spector, who produced many of the hits for these new stars, including "To Know Him Is to Love Him" (1958), "Corinna, Corinna" (1960), "Da Doo Ron Ron" (1963), and "Then He Kissed Me" (1963).

In addition to the Shirelles, the girl groups included the Chantels, the Chiffons, the Ronettes, the Dixie Cups, the Crystals, the Shangri-Las, Martha and the Vandellas, Rosie and the Originals, the Angels, the Marvelettes, and the Cookies. In 1961 the Top Ten included "Angel Baby" (Rosie and the Originals) and "Please Mr. Postman" (Marvelettes) as well as the hits by the Shirelles.

Of all the girl groups, one stands out. The Supremes were more popular, more financially successful, and more distinctive than all the rest. Just as girl groups were beginning to fade, this black trio from Detroit hit the Top Ten on both charts with "Where Did Our Love Go?" (1964). It was the beginning of a phenomenal career for Diana

Left: *The Shirelles were one of the few girl groups to record hits they wrote themselves.* Facing page: *Did the Supremes ever perform "Stop! In the Name of Love" without making this famous gesture?*

The Ronettes, with lead singer Ronnie Bennett in the middle. The group was named, produced, and managed by Bennett's husband-to-be, Phil Spector.

Ross, Mary Wilson, and Florence Ballard. From 1964 to 1969 almost every tune the Supremes sang turned to gold. They had twelve number one hits out of eighteen that made the Top Ten. "Where Did Our Love Go" (1964) was followed in rapid succession by "Baby Love" (1964), "Come See About Me" (1965), "Stop! In the Name of Love" (1965), "Back in My Arms Again" (1965), "I Hear a Symphony" (1965), "You Can't Hurry Love (1966), "You Keep Me Hangin' On" (1966), "Love Is Here and Now You're Gone" (1967), "The Happening" (1967), "Love Child" (1968), and "Someday We'll Be Together" (1969).

The Supremes showed just how far black groups had come since the segregated days of the early 1950s. All three singers had been raised in the Brewster Housing Project in Detroit; all three grew up with gospel, rhythm and blues, and early rock music. In an interview in *Time* in 1966 Diana Ross mused on their success: "You know, we used to get excited about the Apollo [a famous black nightclub]. We never even thought about the Copa [a famous white nightclub]." Although success would be fleeting for Wilson and Ballard, Diana Ross used her beginnings with the Supremes as a springboard to a career that embraced Hollywood and television, as well as solo hit records.

The Supremes were one part of Motown, the most famous and probably most profitable black recording label in the world. In the 1960s Motown represented the extent to which black musicians had knocked over the color barrier that had been keeping them from national recognition and financial success.

The brainchild of a songwriter named Berry Gordy, Motown's first contracts included Smokey Robinson and the Miracles, the Marvelettes, and Marvin Gaye. Gordy kept a tight rein on his artists. For the most part they sang songs written for them by the team of Brian Holland, Lamont Dozier, and Eddie Holland. Between 1963 and 1966 Motown artists recorded dozens of Top Ten hits. The Motown sound was easily recognizable, whether the singers were the Supremes, Gladys Knight and the Pips, the Four Tops, Jr. Walker and the All Stars, or Martha and the Vandellas. As *The Rolling Stone History of Rock and Roll* has analyzed them, Motown hits were characterized by repeated refrains of a song's hook line, "gospelish vocal gestures," "hot" instrumentals designed to "make a song jump out of a car window," and a 4-4 beat.

Marvin Gaye, prince of the Motown empire

Motown records had an extraordinary hit ratio (number of hit songs per number recorded), reaching an all-time high of 75 percent in 1966. By the late 1960s Gordy's company ranked among the most successful black-owned corporations in America. The Motown sound established once and for all the place of black musicians in the center of mainstream American music.

At the same time that Motown was joyously bringing black music to the forefront of American popular tastes, another group scored with hit after hit set in a world far removed from the black urban scene. The Beach Boys captured the charts with songs of sun and surf and California. Three brothers, Brian, Carl, and Dennis Wilson, along with Mike Love and Alan Jardine, made up the original group (shown at left). They fit the era because they were young, good-looking males who sang about teenage love and cars and fun. They would outlast other teen idols, however, and for the most part, the music they made was their own. In the early days they sang mostly of surfing, a subject that was so popular that kids who had never seen the ocean enthused about "catching a wave."

In 1963 the Beach Boys made the Top Ten with "Surfin' USA." They followed this hit with twelve other Top Ten singles in the next three years, including: "Surfer Girl" (1963), "Fun, Fun, Fun" (1964), "Help Me Rhonda" (1965), and "Good Vibrations" (1966). Although they had one more Top Ten success a decade later, they are best identified with the teen sound of early sixties rock and roll.

Between 1958, when Elvis was inducted into the army, and 1964, when the Beatles hit the United States, rock and roll music was the preserve of teenage audiences and male-dominated recording studios. Some of the songs and sounds produced during these years were memorable, others were not. Almost all are instantly recognizable as belonging to an era of innocence—before rock and roll turned to rock, before the United States became enmeshed in Vietnam, before teenagers sought their thrills in drugs.

CHAPTER FOUR

THE BRITISH INVADE ROCK

THE POP REVOLUTION

For British teenagers, unlike their American counterparts, the 1950s were not a decade of quick retreat to peaceful prosperity. Part of World War II had been fought in Great Britain. Hitler's airplanes had bombed London and other major industrial areas. The 1950s were years of rebuilding. British life was grim, and money, food, and other basic necessities were scarce. As American baby boomers graduated from bubble gum, Davy Crockett, and hula hoops to rock and roll, British kids envied them, unable to share in the postwar luxuries of the United States.

By 1960, however, the British economy was rallying, the wartime damage had been mostly repaired, and British youth were anxious to swing into the rock and roll scene. The place to score was still America. Teenagers had more money in America, and consequently, record sales were bigger there. Young British musicians had followed the careers of Chuck Berry, Elvis Presley, Little Richard, and the pop singers of the late fifties. Their accents might be British but their sounds were a mixture of American country and American rhythm and blues—in short, rock and roll sounds.

In 1963 a phenomenon that would come to be known as "Beatlemania" swept through Great Britain. The objects of the craze were four young men with unfashionably—though not for long—shaggy hair curling over the backs of their necks. Their names were John,

*Mass hysteria greeted the Beatles on their first U.S. tour
in 1964. John Lennon later claimed, "We're bigger than Jesus."*

Paul, George, and Ringo. As a quartet they had played together, with limited success, since 1962. Paul and John had known each other since boyhood, however, and with a series of musicians, including George after 1958, had been known as the Quarrymen and the Silver Beatles before settling on the Beatles in 1960.

John Lennon, Paul McCartney, George Harrison, and Ringo Starr (nee Richard Starkey, Jr.) had been born within three years of each other in Liverpool, England. Ringo was the oldest, born July 7, 1940, and George was the youngest, born February 25, 1943. They were all raised in solid, lower-middle-class homes by parents caught up in England's struggle to recover from the war years. None of the four had much formal education, and all had been playing in bands since their teens. John Lennon would emerge as their leader, and he and Paul McCartney wrote much of the group's best music. John played the guitar, keyboard instruments, and the harmonica. Paul played the bass, guitar, and keyboards. George played the guitar and, later, the sitar. Ringo played the drums. All four sang.

"Please Please Me" made the number one position on the charts in Great Britain in 1963. Released in the United States at the same time, the song never even made it to the Top 100. In fact, until February 1964, no Beatles tune climbed anywhere near the top of the Billboard charts in America. Then, overnight, "I Want to Hold Your Hand" hit number one, with "She Loves You" in the number three spot. By February, one month later, "She Loves You" was in the first position, "I Want to Hold Your Hand" was second, "Please Please Me" was third, and "Twist and Shout" claimed the eighth position. Four hits on the Top Ten simultaneously—not even Elvis had matched that record. By April, five Beatles songs would rank in the top ten.

In 1964 seven more Beatles numbers hit the Top Ten: "Can't Buy Me Love," "Love Me Do," "A Hard Day's Night," "I Feel Fine," "Do You Want to Know a Secret," and "She's a Woman." Nineteen sixty-four was truly the Beatles' year. They took America by storm, appearing on two highly publicized segments of the "Ed Sullivan Show," singing, laughing, shaking their mopheads, and generally looking as though they were having fun. For a group that would be credited with sparking a cultural revolution, the Beatles in their early years seemed, with the exception of their hair length, exceedingly nonrevolutionary. Their songs were mostly about young love, with mass-market lyrics that could have come straight from the pens of the Brill Building hit writers. The most distinguishing characteristic of their music was its beat—big and loud. In reviewing one of their early performances, the *New York Times* called the Beatles "one-tenth hair, one-tenth music and eight-tenths publicity."

Part of what set the early Beatles apart from the groups that came later was the very fact that most of their music was not written by anyone else. They were not just performers. They prided themselves on following the tradition of early blues and rhythm artists who wrote and recorded their own music. One or another of the four credited Chuck Berry, Little Richard, Buddy Holly, and Chet Atkins with influencing his style. After the Beatles, nearly all important rock and roll music was written by the artists who performed it.

Rolling Stone has called the Beatles phenomenon a "pop explosion." The Beatles were central figures in the popular revolution in manners and morals that took place in American society in the 1960s. Their appearance on the Billboard charts took place a very short time after the assassination of President John F. Kennedy, an event that signaled an irrecoverable loss of innocence for the American public. During the decade of the Beatles' greatest popularity, America would lose its first war (in Vietnam) and would become thoroughly bitter about and disenchanted with its political leaders. Accompanying all these changes was a basic change in morality: the "sexual revolution." Music did not cause this revolution—certainly the Beatles singing about the joys of holding hands did not cause this revolution—but the Beatles and other rock and roll groups focused on the new morality and their lyrics celebrated the outermost boundaries of social change.

The Beatles changed with the times, and it is their flexibility that will undoubtedly preserve their place in music history. The four good-time Charlies who sang "Love Me Do," and who seemed naively happy that people liked their music so much that they got rich, became more and more serious musicians. By 1967 the Beatles were experimenting with new forms of instrumentation, new lyrics, and new themes. Like other groups they toyed with the world of psychedelic drugs. By the late sixties and early seventies, even as they were breaking up as a group, their music carried universal messages of peace and of environmental concern.

The haircuts were everywhere: on Beatle dolls, Beatle wigs, Beatle lunchboxes, and the Beatles cartoon show. Below: *The Beatles at the time the* Sgt. Pepper's Lonely Hearts Club Band *album was released*

Between 1964 and 1970 sixteen Beatles singles made number one on the Top Ten. Because it was being sung by the Beatles, a schmaltzy ballad like "Yesterday" (number one in 1965) classified as rock music. Other top tunes had a more recognizable Beatles beat: "Eight Days a Week" (1965), "Ticket to Ride" (1965), "Help" (1965), and "We Can Work It Out" (1965). After 1966 their hits were mellower: "Paperback Writer" (1966), "All You Need Is Love" (1967), "Penny Lane" (1967), "Hello Goodbye" (1968), "Hey Jude" (1968), "Let It Be" (1970), and their final number one hit as a complete quartet, "The Long and Winding Road" (1970).

In 1970 the album *McCartney* was released. A solo effort by Paul, this album signaled the end of the Beatles as a group. George, John, and Ringo followed Paul's example and recorded singles and albums on their own. John, along with his wife, Yoko Ono, was perhaps the most famous outside the group, but Paul sold the greatest number of records. Until John's assassination in 1980, Beatles fans harbored the not-so-secret wish that the foursome would get together one more time. A bullet fired by a disturbed youth on December 8, 1980, ended that hope forever.

The Beatles were part, the most important part, of a general wave of British groups washing over the United States in the mid-1960s. Dubbed the "British Invasion," this movement saw the rise and fall of countless rock groups. Those, like the Beatles, who hailed from Liverpool developed the "Mersey beat," so called because of the Mersey River flowing by that city. Mersey beat groups included the Searchers, the Merseybeats, and Gerry and the Pacemakers. Lest there be any doubt of their association with Liverpool, this last group's biggest hit was "Ferry Across the Mersey" (1965).

Manchester, England, was another industrial city producing international musicians. Out of Manchester came the Hollies, Freddie and the Dreamers, and Wayne Fontana and the Mindbenders. The Hollies' biggest early hit was "Bus Stop" (1966), a light, quirky tune squarely in the middle of early Beatles tradition. Freddie and the Dreamers contributed a number one hit in 1965. "I'm Telling You Now," and added one more oddly named dance to the fads of the early sixties—"The Freddie." Wayne Fontana and his group scored with "Game of Love" in 1965.

Other British groups successful in the race to the top of the

American charts included the Dave Clark Five, the Animals, Herman's Hermits, the Moody Blues, and the Yardbirds. Dave Clark's enthusiastic sound was rhythmic and cheerful and great for dancing. Although only one of the group's songs made it to number one, "Over and Over" (1966), the group had six other hits in 1964 and 1965. "Glad All Over," "Bits and Pieces," "Can't You See That She's Mine," "Because," "I Like It Like That," and "Catch Us If You Can" were all Top Ten singles.

During these same years the Animals, under the leadershp of Eric Burdon, had big hits with "The House of the Rising Sun" (1964) and "C.C. Rider" (1966). The Yardbirds contributed "For Your Love" and "Heart Full of Soul" in 1965. In terms of sheer numbers of hits, however, the most successful of the lesser British Invasion groups in the mid-sixties was Herman's Hermits. Led by Peter "Herman" Noone, the Hermits had a clean-cut look, in spite of their fashionably long hair. The one word that best describes most of their songs is "cute." Even the titles were cute, the cutest being the number one hit "I'm Henry VIII, I Am." Herman's Hermits were decidedly British; unlike many of the English groups who affected country drawls, their British accents came through clearly on their records. Between 1965 and 1967 the group had ten hits in addition to "Henry VIII." Only "Mrs. Brown You've Got a Lovely Daughter" (1965) hit number one, but the others were strong sellers with wide audience appeal. In 1965 they included "Can't You Hear My Heartbeat," "Silhouettes," "Wonderful World," and "Just a Little Bit Better." In 1966 "A Must to Avoid," "Listen People," "Leaning on the Lamp Post," and "Dandy" made the charts. The group's last big hit, "There's a Kind of Hush," came in 1967.

Single female vocalists and male duos were also part of the British invasion. Dusty Springfield and Petula Clark belong to this tradition, as do Chad and Jeremy and Peter and Gordon. Clark boasted two number one singles, "Downtown" (1965) and "My Love" (1966), and a host of lesser hits. Dusty Springfield never had a number one single, but her two songs "Wishin' and Hopin' " (1964) and "You Don't Have to Say You Love Me" (1966) were hits. In 1964 Chad and Jeremy sang "A Summer Song" and Peter and Gordon were number one with "A World without Love." Peter and Gordon had two more Top Ten hits, "I Go to Pieces" (1965) and "Lady Godiva" (1966).

With the success of the Beatles, all things British became fashionable. Clockwise from top: *Gerry and the Pacemakers, Herman's Hermits, Peter and Gordon, and Petula Clark*

Joining these groups after 1965 was a second wave of bands, some from Great Britain, and all characterized by the British sound. Near the end of the decade the Bee Gees, a group from Australia, began a series of hits that would last through the seventies as they bridged the gap from the Beatles to disco. In the United States, record producers, much as they had capitalized on Elvis look-alikes in the late fifties, manufactured Beatle look-alikes in the sixties. One of the most successful of the artificially created groups was the Monkees. Composed of one honest-to-goodness Englishman, Davy Jones, one television actor, Mickey Dolenz, and two small-time musicians, Peter Tork and Mike Nesmith, the Monkees played their instruments so poorly that their records rarely included any of their own instrumentation. Nevertheless, Nesmith was a bona fide songwriter and the Monkees sold records largely because of the success of their popular TV series, "The Monkees." Between 1966 and 1968 the Monkees had three number one hits: "Last Train to Clarksville" (1966), "I'm a Believer" (1967), and "Daydream Believer" (1968).

The Monkees

*Mick Jagger of the
Rolling Stones flaunting
the best-known lips in
rock and roll*

Many of the groups who were part of the British Invasion passed quickly from the scene. Besides the Beatles, only one group was truly revolutionary. These were the Rolling Stones. Unlike the Beatles, for whom music was a way to break out of the poverty of their youth, the Stones were not especially poor. Their leader, Mick Jagger, was a student at the London School of Economics before he became a full-time musician.

If the Beatles came to symbolize a lot of the cultural revolution of the 1960s, the Rolling Stones did everything they could to push that revolution even further. Their sexuality was explicit and their violence was legion. They were loud, often vulgar, and had the longest hair yet. In an era of changing conventions, they seemed always to be on the cutting edge. Mick Jagger was sexy and sensual, and the group's 1967 hit "Let's Spend the Night Together" was far more outspoken than any popular song previously recorded. The original Rolling Stones included Mick Jagger, vocalist and group leader, Keith Richards and Brian Jones on guitar, Bill Wyman on bass, and Charlie Watts on drums.

The Rolling Stones' first number one hit on the popular charts was their 1965 smash, the less-than-subtle "(I Can't Get No) Satisfaction." Throughout the sixties the Stones had thirteen songs make the Top Ten, with "Get Off My Cloud" (1965), "Paint It Black" (1966), "Ruby Tuesday" (1967), and "Honky Tonk Woman" (1969) all spending time in the number one spot.

The Rolling Stones continued to record hit songs throughout the seventies. They counted on their rebelliousness to attract youthful audiences looking for antiheroes. Between 1971 and 1980 "Brown Sugar" (1971), "Angie" (1973), "Fool to Cry" (1976), "Beast of Burden" (1978), and "Emotional Rescue" (1980) were Top Ten singles. Their albums from this decade met with popular success also, although some people found their content in questionable taste.

The entrance of the Rolling Stones into the world of popular music signaled a major shift in the history of rock and roll. The Beatles bridged the gap between teenybopper love songs and the protest music of the late sixties, but the Stones never presented a clean-cut image. Significantly, their badness sold records. With the Stones' explicit lyrics about drugs and antiauthoritarianism, the flaunting of tradition and sexual freedom moved via hit records into the mainstream of teenage culture.

CHAPTER FIVE

ROCK AND ROLL AND THE COUNTERCULTURE

PROTEST AND DRUGS

In 1965 Lyndon Johnson was inaugurated as the thirty-sixth president of the United States. Many people voted for him only because they feared that Barry Goldwater, his Republican opponent, was more likely to start a nuclear war. In 1965 Martin Luther King, Jr., led four thousand supporters in a civil rights march from Selma to Montgomery, Alabama; the Ku Klux Klan shot at the civil rights workers in Selma. In 1965 *The Green Berets*, a novel glorifying the American commando unit operating in Southeast Asia, made the best-seller lists. And in 1965 Vietnamese planes shot down United States aircraft and student protesters in Washington, D.C., held the first of many antiwar demonstrations.

In September 1965 "Eve of Destruction," recorded by Barry McGuire, was number three on Billboard's Top Ten. Written by P. F. Sloan, a young man barely out of his teens, "Eve of Destruction" described the chaos in the world and the youthful frustration at the mess things were in—a mess blamed on adult mishandling of politics, foreign affairs, and human relations. Sang McGuire, "The Eastern World, it is explodin'. . . . You're old enough to kill, but not for votin'."

"Eve of Destruction" was one of the more graphic numbers in a long line of protest songs. For many years American folk music had been connected with political and social protest. The fight against slavery, the battle for unionization, and the struggle against racism had all had their battle songs. Woody Guthrie and Pete Seeger had built folk careers on solo guitar pieces chronicling American democracy and extolling the dignity of the individual in a majority culture that too often violated minority rights. In spite of the movement toward rock and roll music in the 1950s, the folk tradition had remained a steady, quiet strand in the musical world, usually classified with country and western.

Folk music merged with rock and roll in the mid-sixties when several young artists began to write and perform rock music with a folk message. Fueled by the civil rights movement and the war in Vietnam, songwriters and singers used rock and roll music to protest racism and war. Rock and roll was so much a part of American culture, especially youth culture, that it was seen as the perfect medium through which to send the antiwar message.

The chief folk rock musician was Bob Dylan. Originally a pure folk singer in the Woodie Guthrie tradition, Dylan outraged many people in the audience at the 1965 Newport Folk Festival when he added rock to his performance. Once Dylan turned to rock, folk music was never the same again.

Born Robert Zimmerman in 1941, Dylan has been called "the most influential American pop musician of the sixties." He arranged to meet his idol, Woody Guthrie, in 1961, and in the early 1960s was strongly influenced by Joan Baez, a folk singer who had already established her reputation as an activist. The title of Dylan's 1964 album, *The Times They Are A-Changin'*, foreshadowed the political and cultural upheaval that would shake up the nation during the Vietnam years.

Dylan hit the popular charts in September 1965 with his single "Like a Rolling Stone." Just a few months before, another folk rock number, written by Bob Dylan, had climbed to number three on the Top Ten. This was "Mr. Tambourine Man," performed by the Byrds. These two songs shared the top of the charts with cheery British Invasion tunes such as "Mrs. Brown You've Got a Lovely Daughter" (Herman's Hermits), Motown hits like the Four Tops' "I Can't Help Myself," and surfing music from the Beach Boys ("California Girls"). Nevertheless, change was in the air. Rioting in the black ghettos of

American cities and escalation of the war in Vietnam would both intensify after 1965. As the world seemingly became more chaotic, the songs protesting the causes of the chaos became more numerous and more popular.

The Byrds were at the peak of their popularity during these years. Led by the guitar-playing vocalist Roger McGuinn, the band numbered four musicians. Chris Hillman, Gene Clark, and David Crosby all helped out with the singing as well as playing their individual instruments—the bass, tambourine/guitar, and guitar, respectively. They followed up "Mr. Tambourine Man" with a number one hit in 1966, "Turn, Turn, Turn." The lyrics of this classic folk rock tune came from the Bible, the music was originally composed by Pete Seeger, and the Byrds added rock instrumentation.

Other folk rock musicians included the Lovin' Spoonful, the Mamas and the Papas, the Turtles, Donovan, Sonny and Cher, and Buffalo Springfield. Artists like Peter, Paul, and Mary, who had begun their careers as pure folksingers in Greenwich Village cafés, now turned to the rock sound. The Lovin' Spoonful had a series of Top Ten hits, including a number one tune, "Summer in the City" (1966). The Turtles hit the top of the charts with "Happy Together" (1967), and both the Turtles and Sonny and Cher sang "It Ain't Me Babe." Sonny and Cher tended to focus on the idea that the love of an individual couple provided the only stability in a changing world. This was the theme of their biggest hit, "I Got You Babe" (1965), and of "All I Ever Need Is You" (1971).

Left: *Bob Dylan in 1976. When he first performed live on electric guitar in 1965, Dylan shocked folk music traditionalists and instantaneously invented folk rock.* Top right: *Acoustic folkies Peter, Paul and Mary.* Bottom right: *The singing duo of Salvatore Bono and his wife, Cherilyn Sarkasian LaPier, better known as Sonny and Cher.*

The Fifth Dimension

James Brown—also known as J.B., Soul Brother Number One, the Godfather of Soul, and the Hardest Working Man in Show Business—performing in 1965

The theme of love was closely tied to the theme of peace. As the antiwar demonstrations continued, musicians emphasized love and flowers as an alternative to war and guns. Groups like the Fifth Dimension sang protest songs based on love and utopia. The Fifth Dimension's first number one hit came from the rock musical *Hair*. *Hair* captured the look of the decade—long hair as a protest against societal conventions, flower power as a protest against military power. The lyrics of its songs were antiestablishment, antimilitary, pro-love and pro–sexual freedom. "The Age of Aquarius" that the Fifth Dimension sang about in 1969 heralded a new age in which "peace will guide the planets and love will steer the stars."

Peace was the leading message of the late sixties, but the decade also saw music with another social message. Early in his career Bob Dylan sang "The Lonely Death of Hattie Carroll," a protest against racism. However, it was the black soul singers of the mid-1960s who embodied the civil rights movement in their music. Soul was the music of black pride. Soul music aptly fit the early sixties, the civil rights era. As the civil rights movement urged black Americans to be proud of their heritage, soul hit the charts; it was music that celebrated black musical roots, especially gospel and blues. Soul sang of the heartland of black America.

A combination of gospel, blues, country, and rock, soul reached its greatest heights with artists like Otis Redding, James Brown, Ray Charles, Wilson Pickett, and Aretha Franklin. Most soul music was recorded on the Atlantic label. Atlantic was the company of Otis Redding, Wilson Pickett, and James Brown. Franklin was the uncontested Queen of Soul. Her Top Ten hits began in 1967 with "I Never Loved a Man (The Way I Love You)."

The soul of the sixties differed from earlier soul music because of its strong rock beat. Wilson Pickett's "In the Midnight Hour" (1965) and Percy Sledge's "When a Man Loves a Woman" (1966) were classic soul hits. The popularity of black soul music emphasized, along with Motown, the increasing integration of black music into American popular music. Soul died with the assassination of Martin Luther King, Jr., in 1968. The optimism that characterized soul was destroyed by King's murder. Pure soul was superseded by a tougher form of black music that revealed the anger felt by many black Americans in the late sixties and into the seventies.

Right: *Aretha Franklin's best-loved classic may be her version of Otis Redding's "Respect."* Bottom: *Sly and the Family Stone mixed soul music's dance rhythm with a rock band's raw power and the result was called "funk."*

Some of the most exciting soul was produced by Sly Stone. In 1968 Sly and the Family Stone recorded "Dance to the Music." This was followed by "I Want to Take You Higher" (1969), "Hot Fun in the Summertime" (1969), and "Thank You Falettinme Be Mice Elf Again" (1970). Other veterans of the soul scene also sang songs symptomatic of black frustration with the decade of Cambodia and Watergate. Marvin Gaye recorded "What's Going On" (1971) and the O'Jays had a hit with "Backstabbers" (1972).

The attack on the conventions of society unleashed a feeling that everything the older generation stood for was wrong. There was widespread agreement among rock and roll performers and their youthful audiences that a generation that had lied about Vietnam must have lied about everything else. This mistrust of the adult generation contributed to the growth of the drug culture. Drugs signaled the ultimate rejection of whatever the older generation stood for.

The Beatles, the Rolling Stones, and Bob Dylan all experimented with and sang about drugs in the late sixties. The songs they sang had immense popularity and may have influenced the spread of drugs throughout the youth culture of America. In 1966 Bob Dylan sang "Ev'rybody must get stoned," and his songs were banned by some radio stations. That same year he had a Top Ten hit with "Rainy Day Women," a slang term for marijuana. In reviewing this song, *Time* magazine commented on the "spate of new songs dealing with all kinds of taboo topics." To the older generation rock music often seemed synonymous with the drug culture.

In 1967 a singer named Scott McKenzie had his only career Top Ten hit with "San Francisco," a song written by Papa John Phillips (of the Mamas and the Papas). McKenzie advised, "If you're going to San Francisco, be sure to wear some flowers in your hair." By the late sixties San Francisco had become not only the center of love and peace music, but also the center of the drug scene. The coming together of these two forces in rock and roll reinforced the fears of adults that rock and drugs were inseparable. For musicians, however, the psychedelic drugs encouraged new creativity and pushed them beyond the bounds of conventional expression. Chet Helms, the manager of the Avalon Ballroom, a popular place for rock concerts in San Francisco, explained the uniqueness of the "San Francisco sound'' as stemming from ''the growing influence of psychedelic chemicals as a tool for expression.'' The sound was loud, unconventional, and often compelling. As one critic described it, the San Francisco sound was characterized by long songs, ''often fifteen minutes or longer, ample time to build thunderous climax upon climax; to change the throbbing tempos, and within a single number to pass through the land of the blues, the folk, the country and anywhere else. . . .''

By 1966 it was estimated that there were fifteen hundred bands in the San Francisco area. Among those with national reputations were Big Brother and the Holding Company, Quicksilver Messenger Service, the Sopwith Camel, the 13th Floor Elevators, Country Joe and the Fish, and Loading Zone. By far the most sucessful, however, were the Jefferson Airplane (now Jefferson Starship) and the Grateful Dead.

In the beginning the Dead played only for live audiences; they believed that their music could best be experienced when accompanied by drug use, by both the band and the audience. Grateful Dead fans, calling themselves the Dead Heads, were devoted to the band and to drugs. As *Rolling Stone* analyzed their music, ''the lyrics and the special sound effects recreated aspects of the psychedelic experience—revelatory roaring, chills of ecstasy, hallucinated wandering, mystico-psychotic wonder. . . .'' To those who did not share the enthusiasm of the Dead Heads, the music was just boring.

Above: Jefferson Airplane symbolized the hippie scene of the Haight-Ashbury district in San Francisco. From left to right: Marty Balin, Grace Slick, Spencer Dryden, Paul Kantner, Jorma Kaukonen, and Jack Casady. Below: The line-up of the Grateful Dead has changed over the years as its members quit or died. Shown here is the Dead in the early 1980s.

New music forms were all part of the revolt against established customs and the older generation. The antiauthoritarian protest feeling was perhaps captured best at a number of giant rock concerts that symbolized the solidarity of youth in support of peace and rock music. In June 1967 the first rock concert was held in Monterey, California. Dubbed the Monterey International Pop Festival, the gathering attracted over fifty thousand people, most of them without tickets. The slogan for the event was "music, love and flowers," and the performers ranged from Jimi Hendrix and Janis Joplin to Simon and Garfunkel, Otis Redding, and the Mamas and the Papas.

The greatest rock festival of all time occurred in August 1969 near the tiny New York farm village of Bethel. Over four hundred thousand people jammed the Woodstock Music and Arts Festival. There were shortages of food, water, bathrooms, and shelter, but Woodstock became synonymous with cooperative communal gatherings.

Folk singers such as Joan Baez and Arlo Guthrie shared the stage with the Who, the Grateful Dead, Blood, Sweat, and Tears, and Jimi Hendrix. For the next few years promoters would try to duplicate Woodstock. However, the mass gatherings in other places, particularly at Altamont, led too often to violence and sometimes death.

There was a positive side to the rock concerts, however. The Monterey festival had produced $200,000 to be contributed to charity. While some rock concerts were purely commercial ventures designed to make money for star performers and the producers, many had charitable goals. The rock concert as a political forum and fund-raiser is an idea that has survived into the 1980s.

The scene at Woodstock.
Inset: *Stephen Stills and David Crosby of Crosby, Stills, Nash and Young. The band had played only two concerts together before taking the stage at Woodstock.*

CHAPTER SIX

THE 1970s

THE FRAGMENTATION
OF ROCK

Throughout 1970 the Top Ten included hits by the Supremes ("Someday We'll Be Together"), Peter, Paul, and Mary ("Leavin' on a Jet Plane"), Elvis Presley ("Don't Cry Daddy"), the Beatles ("Let It Be"), the Hollies ("He Ain't Heavy"), Smokey Robinson and the Miracles ("The Tears of a Clown"), and Chicago ("Does Anybody Really Know What Time It Is"). The music was diverse, but easily recognizable as part of the first fifteen years of rock and roll. Rockabilly, the British invasion, folk rock, Motown, and country rock were all represented.

In 1980 the Top Ten artists for the year included Michael Jackson, Blondie, Pink Floyd, Captain and Tennille, Queen, Paul McCartney, and Billy Joel. Joel's biggest hit for the year was titled "It's Still Rock and Roll to Me." The words capture the spirit of rock music during the decade of the seventies. In the ten years between 1970 and 1980, rock music splintered in many different directions, but it was still rock and roll, whether it was a solo number by Kenny Loggins or Christopher Cross or a group number by the Spinners, Queen, or Air Supply.

In the 1970s there was no single cause around which rock musicians rallied. Watergate merely confirmed the cynicism of the younger generation, a cynicism that had been born during Vietnam. Furthermore, the majority of the population was no longer teenaged. With each passing year the Baby Boomers, America's single largest population segment, grew older. In the seventies they were in their twenties and beginning to settle down with families and careers. As their lives shifted, so did their musical tastes. Meanwhile, smaller groups of young people supported a variety of different styles of rock.

By 1970 the rock music audience had already begun to fragment. The divisions included those who listened to AM radio and those who patronized FM; those who were in college and those who were still in high school; those who believed in hardcore rock and those who liked "bubble gum rock." Perhaps the most popular band in America at the start of the decade was Creedence Clearwater Revival. Under the direction of John Fogerty, they managed to bridge many of the gaps. *Rolling Stone* commented, "Creedence dominated Top Forty radio for two years without disappointing the anticommercial element of the rock audience." Their first gold single was "Proud Mary." They went on to have six more Top Ten singles in 1970 and 1971.

Most musicians of the 1970s, however, were not as successful as Creedence in attracting the support and attention of all segments of the rock audience. One of the very distinctive new elements of this era was the sound that came to be called "heavy metal." Popularized by Led Zeppelin early in the decade, heavy metal was a unique sound that traced its roots to the Who and the guitar innovations of Eric Clapton and Jeff Beck. Heavy metal was loud, distorted, and primal. Its harshest critics claimed that no matter what band was playing what sound, all heavy metal recordings were indistinguishable from each other.

The members of Kiss never appeared in public without their makeup.

Nevertheless, heavy metal groups like Led Zeppelin, Deep Purple, Kiss, and Alice Cooper all had Top Ten hits in the seventies. Grand Funk Railroad hit the top of the charts twice with "We're an American Band" (1973) and "The Loco-Motion" (1974). Perhaps the best description of heavy metal comes from Lester Bangs, music critic for *Rolling Stone* and *The Village Voice*: "Its noise is created by electric guitars, filtered through an array of warping devices from fuzz-tone to wah-wah, cranked several decibels past the pain threshold, loud enough to rebound off the walls of the biggest arenas anywhere." By the late seventies, heavy metal had lost most of its audience, but it would see a resurgence in popularity with the advent of MTV.

That segment of the teenage audience that had rallied to the heavy metal sound moved next to punk rock, one of the most controversial of all rock and roll genres. Punk, which developed in Great Britain, was a reaction to the perception that rock music had become the property of the establishment.

Punk rock is the clearest expression of antisocial feeling ever to exist in rock music. Punk presents new lyrics and fresh music, but is often brutal and violent. In July 1977 the Ramones recorded the first punk single to hit the Billboard Top 100. (No punk number had ever hit the Top Ten.) *Time* magazine reviewed punk music in an article titled "Anthems of the Blank Generation," and *The New Republic* commented about punk in 1979, that "the lyrics are spit up from a roiling mass of guitars, globs of venom from the bowels of a viper."

In spite of the condemnation by the older generation, punk found a following. By far the most famous—or infamous—of the punkers were Johnny Rotten and Sid Vicious of the Sex Pistols. The Sex Pistols' first single was titled "Anarchy in the U.K.," its very name an expression of the group's philosophy. Before the Sex Pistols were finished as a group (Rotten quit the group and Vicious died of a heroin overdose), they had repulsed many of their listeners.

Not all punk groups were as extreme as the Sex Pistols. The Clash, formed by Joe Strummer, Mick Jones, and Paul Simonon in 1976, was a more mainstream punk band. Although always on the cutting edge politically and musically, the Clash did not go off the deep end into violence as some other punk groups did.

*The Sex Pistols (left to right): Paul Cook,
Sid Vicious, Johnny Rotten, and Steve Jones.
Sang Rotten, "I want to be in anarchy."*

Funk rhymes with punk, and funk was a part of the 1970s, too. There the similarities stop. Funk was the black music of the seventies. As had happened with other forms of rock and roll, soul had grown older along with its audience. Funk was born as the music of the young urban blacks. It was, said *Rolling Stone*, "the inner city sound of exhilaration and ecstasy." Earth, Wind, and Fire and Kool and the Gang were two of the funkiest bands around. Between 1974 and 1980, Earth, Wind, and Fire had six Top Ten singles and thirteen hits on the Rhythm and Blues charts. "Shining Star" (1975), "Sing a Song" (1976), "Got to Get You into My Life" (1978), "September" (1979), "Boogie Wonderland" (1979), and "After the Love Has Gone" (1979) all ranked in the Top Ten on both charts. Earth, Wind, and Fire used all the traditions of the black musical heritage to create their sound, from gospel to Latin rhythms to falsetto vocals.

Contemporaries of Earth, Wind, and Fire, Kool and the Gang was another funky group. They, too, scored simultaneous hits on the Popular and the Rhythm and Blues charts, but their greatest number of hits were in the rhythm and blues category. They were first heard in 1974 with the hits "Jungle Boogie" and "Hollywood Swinging." After a brief eclipse, they made a strong comeback with disco hits at the end of the seventies, particularly with "Ladies' Night."

In the mid-1970s, between funk and disco, a number of British and American performers wrote and played individualistic music that is best described by the term "New Wave." New Wave music in England was characterized by small recording companies and a variety of punk music styles combined with traditional rock and roll themes. Among its practitioners were Graham Parker, Nick Lowe, and Elvis Costello. Although British New Wave rebelled in part against the commercial success of big American rock and roll groups, there were American New Wave artists as well. The leading peformer and writer of this movement was Jonathan Richman.

Funk was a logical lead-in to disco, because both were essentially urban. Disco turned off pure rock fans because of its slickness and commercialism, but disco is definitely part of the rock music tradition. In 1977 the movie *Saturday Night Fever* focused the country's attention on disco. For a while everyone was dancing to the disco beat. Even hard-core rock groups like the Rolling Stones experimented with songs that had the disco beat.

The New Wave band Talking Heads started their career in 1975 at CBGB, the New York club that also launched Blondie, Television, Patti Smith, and the Ramones.

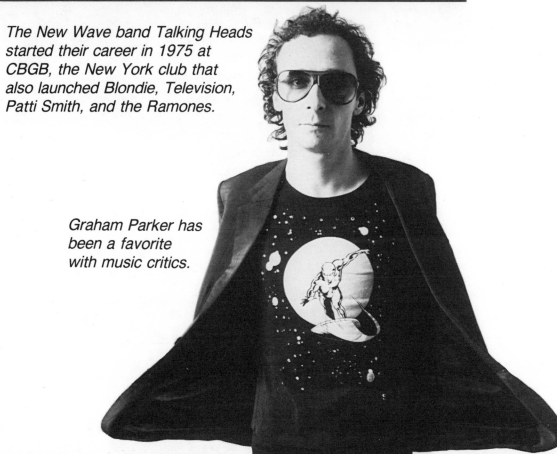

Graham Parker has been a favorite with music critics.

During her
seventeen-minute
song, "Love to
Love You Baby,"
Donna Summer
sang, moaned,
and sighed over
a thundering syn-
thesizer beat.

The Bee Gees'
falsetto voices
were featured
on the sound-
track album of
"Saturday Night
Fever," one of
the biggest-selling
records ever.

Disco was dance music. Not since the mid-1960s had music been so danceable. Whether it was true rock or not seemed irrelevant. It was loud, it had a definite message, and it got people out onto the dance floor like nothing since the sock hop tunes of the late fifties. *Newsweek* defined the disco beat as having "the unaccented regularity of a metronome and the urgency of a war drum." In 1978 twenty of the year's top records were disco tunes.

Like so many forms of rock music, disco owed its existence to black music. Explained *Newsweek*: "From Latin music, [disco] takes its percolating percussion, its sensuous, throbbing rhythms; from the 60s 'funk' music of James Brown and Sly Stone, it borrows a kicky bass-guitar jive; from Afro-Cuban music, it repeats simple lyric lines like voo-doo chants; and like early rock 'n' roll, it exploits the honking saxophones of black rhythm and blues." The reigning queen of disco was Donna Summer. Her classic disco number, "Bad Girls," was a number one hit in 1979. The Bee Gees, the Australian phalanx of the British invasion of the mid-1960s, reentered the limelight as disco stars. "Stayin' Alive," "Night Fever," "Too Much Heaven," and "Tragedy" were all number one hits for the Bee Gees in 1978 and 1979.

In addition to disco, another distinctive branch of rock and roll music emerged from the black tradition in the seventies. This was reggae—Jamaican music. Reggae developed on the island of Jamaica as the musical statement of a group of Jamaicans known as Rastafarians. Worshipers of the late Ethiopian emperor Haile Selassie, the Rastafarians believe that Jamaican culture should reflect its African roots.

Reggae is highly political music, with lyrics that deal with the black heritage of Jamaica and the modern political and social tensions on the small island today. So powerful is reggae for most Jamaicans that Prime Minister Michael Manley used a reggae song, "Better Must Come," as his campaign slogan.

Reggae music developed in Kingston, Jamaica, in the early 1960s. From a small grass-roots musical movement, reggae has grown into one of Jamaica's most important entertainment industries. The local recording companies release over twenty new singles each week, and reggae musicians like Jimmy Cliff, Toots Hibert, and the late Bob Marley are Jamaican superstars. In the United States

Reggae superstar Bob Marley. His death in 1981 was mourned around the world.

and in England such diverse stars as Paul McCartney, Paul Simon, and Eric Clapton have recorded songs with the reggae sound. This is a sound characterized by a guitar that is staccato and scratchy, continual drumming, and a loud bass accompaniment. Reggae emphasizes the first beat, not the second, which is more conventional rock music practice. Often a reggae number will be released twice, once as a vocal and once as a dub. The dub is the instrumental version of the same number and usually consists of five tracks, which gives it a fuller sound.

If the 1970s in rock music were the years when a variety of different musical movements came and went, it was also the decade in which a number of individual musicians, by their innovation and creativity, became musical movements all by themselves. Among these were Peter Frampton, Elton John, and David Bowie. For these musicians, their dynamic stage performances were as compelling as their music and almost as important.

Elton John was born Reginald Kenneth Dwight in England in 1947 and studied from the age of eleven at the Royal Academy of Music. He began his rock and roll career as a songwriter for other people. In 1971 he recorded his first Top Ten hit, "Your Song." At the same time he began to electrify his audience with live concerts that included gymnastics on the piano keyboard. Between 1971 and 1980 Elton John scored fifteen more Top Ten hits, including the number one songs "Crocodile Rock" (1973), "Bennie and the Jets" (1974), his cover of the Beatles song "Lucy in the Sky with Diamonds" (1974), "Philadelphia Freedom" (1975), and "Island Girl" (1975). His hits continued on into the 1980s.

Like Elton John, David Bowie established a reputation for electrifying onstage performances. His outfits rivaled his antics for outrageousness. A big part of each performance was his creation of a character, Ziggy Stardust—a futuristic rock star clad in glittery costumes and topped with a shock of orange hair. In the mid-1970s Bowie dropped Ziggy, but his appearances and his music remained unpredictable. He is credited by *Rolling Stone* for "redefining rebellion as entertainment."

At the same time that Bowie and John were establishing their reputations for flamboyant performances, other singers were bringing a softer sound to rock music. Solo balladeers like Linda Ronstadt, Paul Simon, Neil Young, Carly Simon, and James Taylor recorded a variety of hits throughout the seventies. Some were more popular than rock, some, especially by Ronstadt, were more country than rock, but for the most part these were rock and roll singers whose tunes had mellowed with the times. Typical Top Ten numbers of this type were Carly Simon's "Nobody Does It Better" (1977), James Taylor's "Handy Man" (1977), Paul Simon's number one hit "50 Ways to Leave Your Lover" (1976), and Linda Ronstadt's "It's So Easy" (1977).

One of the most successful bands of the 1970s emerged in 1971 when Glenn Frey and Don Henley left Linda Ronstadt's band to form the Eagles with three other performers. In the summer of 1972 the Eagles had their first Top Ten hit with "Take It Easy." Their biggest success came in 1977 with "Hotel California."

A British band, Fleetwood Mac, matched the commercial success of the Eagles. More widely known in Great Britain than in the

Top left: *Carly Simon sings from the heart and her lyrics are often autobiographical.* Top right: *Linda Ronstadt covered songs by Buddy Holly, Warren Zevon, Chuck Berry, and others, giving them all her mellow, country-influenced sound.* Bottom: *David Bowie, circa 1972, during his Ziggy Stardust phase.* Facing page: *Elton John writes sentimental ballads and rocking pop tunes, and is rarely seen without a pair of large eyeglasses.*

United States during the early part of the decade, Fleetwood Mac gained greater and greater American recognition, finally scoring a number one hit with "Dreams" (1977).

In addition to hits by well-known artists, there was a spate of one-shot records at the top of the charts. Maria Muldaur sang "Midnight at the Oasis" in 1974. Singing about sending your camel to bed seemed no more sophisticated than the lyrics at the end of the 1950s. Ringo Starr had a hit with a remake of the teen classic "You're Sixteen" (1974), and "Smokin' in the Boys' Room" by the Brownville Station (1974) was clearly in the tradition of "Yakety Yak." Helen Reddy and Harry Chapin carried on the folk rock tradition with songs reflecting the social concerns of the decade. Reddy's "I Am Woman" (1972) became the anthem of the feminist movement. Harry Chapin's "Cat's in the Cradle" (1974) chronicled his fears about the emptiness and materialism of modern American life.

Love had always been the single most popular theme of all music, and romantic love returned in the late seventies as the dominant theme in popular rock. Wings sang "Silly Love Songs" in 1976, and it was the number one hit of the year. In 1977 the Emotions made the Top Ten with "Best of My Love." In 1979 Dr. Hook sang "When You're in Love with A Beautiful Woman," and in 1980 Queen considered "The Crazy Little Thing Called Love."

Perhaps the most commercially successful of the new romantic singers was the brother and sister duo, the Carpenters. With Karen on the drums and Richard on the keyboard, they sang mellow, schmaltzy songs that hit the Top Forty and stayed there throughout most of the decade. "Close to You" (1970) was their first number one single; it was followed in rapid succession by other top singles like "Top of the World" (1973) and "Please Mr. Postman" (1975). In 1983 Karen's death from the side effects of anorexia nervosa ended the twosome forever.

As the decade closed, rock music was criticized for having lost its center and focus. To read the charts of the 1970s is to understand this criticism. The music of the decade could not easily be categorized as had the music of earlier periods. But rock and roll—whether pop rock, punk, country rock, reggae, disco, or soft rock—was very much alive and well. Its creativity had stimulated movement in so many directions that it was impossible for any one performer or type of music to command a majority audience for very long.

CHAPTER SEVEN

ROCK MUSIC IN THE REAGAN YEARS

THE MTV CONNECTION

In 1980 a former movie star, Ronald Reagan, was elected president. He understood the popularity of movie stars and rock stars. Michael Jackson and the Beach Boys, among others, made public appearances with the president. In his bid for a second term, Reagan quoted Bruce Springsteen and claimed that the future of America "rests in the message of hope in the songs of a man so many young Americans admire: New Jersey's own Bruce Springsteen." Although Reagan and Springsteen approach most of the nation's problems from opposite ends of the political spectrum, the president's recognition of Springsteen's popularity emphasized once again the centrality of rock and roll music and performers in American culture in 1980.

The overwhelming popularity and success of rock music in the 1980s have been criticized by the purists devoted to the rock and roll of an earlier age. They believe that the music lost its heart and soul when it became big business because big business, after all, represents mainstream America. The powerful, positive side of the commercial success of rock and roll music, however, has been its ability to bring power and success to its performers even when they are not from mainstream groups. Women musicians have been among the beneficiaries of this change.

The 1980s have seen the rise of a series of strong, young female performers who write their own music. Singers like Madonna, Cyndi Lauper, Pat Benatar, Sheila E., Annie Lennox, and Whitney Houston

The Women: (top) Sheila E.,
Madonna, Pat Benatar.
Bottom: *Cyndi Lauper, Annie*
Lennox, Whitney Houston.

© Sheila Escovedo 1986

grew up as the Vietnam years stimulated Americans to challenge old stereotypes. In spite of new acceptance in the sixties and seventies for women as performers, the music industry continued to be dominated by men at all management levels. Today's new women singers, unlike their predecessors, play their own instruments, write much of their own music, and manage their own acts. They are unwilling to be brushed aside as were the girl groups of earlier years.

Cyndi Lauper, with her outlandish outfits and refusal to be like anyone else, was named one of *Ms.* magazine's women of the year for 1984. Lauper claims that a big part of her message is feminist. *Newsweek* quoted her as saying: "I try to beget strength and courage and purpose. I want to show a new woman." The theme of her biggest single, "Girls Just Want to Have Fun," is that women are just as entitled as men to have a good time on their own terms, whatever those terms may be. Lauper's second album, *True Colors*, although not as distinctive as her first, still shot to the top of the charts.

Madonna is the most controversial of the new female singers. The question is whether or not she glorifies the materialism that has long been a target of rock music. Difficult to categorize, Madonna is a strong young woman who has been described by *Time* as an "outrageous blend of Little Orphan Annie, Margaret Thatcher and Mae West." Her best-selling album, *Like a Virgin*, contained five songs that she wrote herself. Her 1985 concert tour, a sellout, was all hers. Not only did she sing and dance, but she managed the entire twenty-eight city tour herself. *True Blue* (1986) moved quickly to the top of the charts, even though songs like "Where's the Party?" and "Jimmy, Jimmy" seemed more like echoes of the girl groups of the 1960s than new 1980s sounds. Madonna is indeed one of the new women, a performer whose career has soared without male management or promotion.

In spite of the success of the new women, a man has dominated the charts in the 1980s. Bruce Springsteen's nickname, "The Boss," reflects his control of the rock music scene. Springsteen sings of the working class; his roots are deep in the rundown New Jersey resort

The Boss

town of Asbury Park. During the late sixties and early seventies, Springsteen started a number of relatively unsuccessful bands before settling with the E Street Band. His first Top Ten hit came in 1979 with "Hungry Heart," but Springsteen's greatest success has come with his personal concerts in the 1980s. Noted for their length, Springsteen's performances are complex and exhausting and have taken him around the world. In 1985 he played before crowds of over seventy thousand throughout Ireland and England. In November of 1986 people stood in line in front of record stores across America waiting for the release of *Bruce Springsteen and the E Street Band Live 1975–1985*, a retrospective of the Boss's career.

Successful as Springsteen is, he is just beginning to approach the unprecedented commercial success of Michael Jackson. Michael Jackson was eleven years old when he and other members of his family were signed by Motown as the Jackson Five. In 1970 the Jackson Five had four number one singles in a row—"I Want You Back," "ABC," "The Love You Save," and "I'll Be There." In 1976 the Jackson Five became the Jacksons, but they continued to record hit songs. In the 1980s, however, the family group was eclipsed by its next-to-the-youngest member, Michael. He branched out on his own, and his first two solo slbums, *Off the Wall* (1979) and *Thriller* (1982), had phenomenal sales and produced numbers of hit singles, including "Rock with You" and "She's Out of My Life" from *Off the Wall* and "Billie Jean" and "Beat It" from *Thriller. Thriller* broke all previous sales records, even those set by Elvis Presley and the Beatles, with sales topping thirty-five million by 1984. By the mid-1980s Jackson made more headlines with his off-beat personal style than with his music. In spite of his eccentricities, however, Jackson can still command huge audiences whenever he performs.

More controversial than Michael Jackson, but highly successful in the 1980s, is Prince. Prince's performances are characterized by

Michael Jackson's electrifying performance of "Billie Jean" on Motown's twenty-fifth anniversary TV special in 1983

outstanding musicianship, erotic songs, and outrageous posturing. He writes most of his own music and plays all the instruments featured on his albums. Although the topics of some of his songs are controversial enough to cause them to be banned from Top Forty airwaves, he has had consistent hits on the Rhythm and Blues charts since the late seventies. In 1982 "Little Red Corvette" was a Top Ten single. His 1987 album, *Sign o' the Times*, also made it into the Top Ten.

The huge success of today's artists in attracting tens of thousands of fans stems in part from their exposure to their audience through video. MTV (Music Television), the single greatest technical innovation of eighties rock, insures maximum publicity for any performers whose videos are played on the twenty-four-hour-a-day channel. Through MTV, rock albums can be visualized. The glitter and color of Madonna, Michael Jackson, and Prince are natural responses to a recording phenomenon that emphasizes what the audience sees as well as what it hears. MTV sells records and makes stars by reaching into well over ten million American homes.

Among the new groups that achieved international stardom in the 1980s, in part because of their videos, are the Cars and Duran, Duran. The American quintet, The Cars, is a New Wave group that owes much of its success to its leader and songwriter, Ric Ocasek. Although the Cars' success is most often measured in terms of their albums—*The Cars* (1978), *Candy-O* (1979), *Panorama* (1981), *Shake It Up* (1981)—they have also scored with hit singles on the Top Forty charts. ("Shake It Up" was number four in 1981.) Duran, Duran, a British group formed in 1978, is similar to the Cars in that their albums have been at least as successful as their singles. Their 1982 hit "Hungry Like the Wolf" established their popularity in the United States, and their lead vocalist, Simon LeBon, became an instant teen idol.

Like their countrymen, Duran, Duran, the Police hit popular Top Forty success by combining old and new rock elements. Their sound incorporates reggae, romance, and Third World rhythms. Their leading songwriter, Sting (Gordon Sumner), played in jazz groups before forming the Police with drummer Stewart Copeland and guitarist Andy Summers. The Police had hits on the Top Ten charts in 1980 and 1981 ("De Do Do Do De Da Da Da," "Don't Stand So Close to Me," "Every Little Thing She Does Is Magic") and a number one hit in 1983 with "Every Breath You Take."

Left: *Some of Prince's biggest hits came from the movies "Purple Rain" and "Under the Cherry Moon," which he wrote and starred in. Below: On the set of MTV with V-J Mark Goodman and Madonna*

Top: *The Cars, a Boston New Wave band.* Left: *The Police began as a punk band and gradually added reggae bass lines, African polyrhythms, and Arab melodies to their music.* Right: *Duran Duran's rise to stardom has closely paralleled the success of MTV.*

A popular duo in the early eighties was the team of Daryl Hall and John Oates. Their sound, created by Oates on guitar and Hall on piano, was a kind of rhythm and blues rock. Hall and Oates' 1981 album, *Private Eyes*, was a huge success; it included two number one singles, "Private Eyes" and "I Can't Go for That (No Can Do)." In 1982 "Maneater" made the Top Forty. At the height of their success, Hall and Oates were characterized by *Billboard* as "the most successful recording duo in history." However, in the mid-1980s the pair split up. Daryl Hall went on to critical acclaim and commercial success with two solo albums, *Sacred Songs* (1985) and *Three Hearts in the Happy Ending Machine* (1986).

Daryl Hall (bottom) and John Oates grew up outside Philadelphia, where they sang in doo-wop rhythm and blues groups.

Another new sound for the mid-eighties is rap music. Rap is more of a chant than a song and is characterized by rapid-fire, staccato conversation against a beat background. Predominantly a black phenomenon, rap was born in the inner cities and its lyrics are usually couched in the vernacular of American urban blacks. Rap has been popularized by such groups as Run-DMC, L. L. Cool J and Whodini. In 1986 Run-DMC hit the top of the charts with the rap album, *Raising Hell*.

Rap music is definitely music of the 1980s. However, the charts of the mid-eighties often include performers who first had hits in the 1960s. For instance, one of the hottest women singers is a performer whose career stretches all the way back to the 1950s when she and her future husband, Ike, made hits that were confined to the then all-black Rhythm and Blues charts. This is Tina Turner. At forty-five years of age she won three Grammy awards for her gold single, "What's Love Got to Do With It?" (1985). Tina Turner has fought racial and sexual oppression for nearly three decades. Her strident voice, her confident, defiant lyrics, her flamboyant appearance, and her astounding financial success after years of poverty all characterize her triumph. Her music gives her the medium to express her message about freedom. As she has said, "Freedom is the secret." Her 1985 album, *Private Dancer*, was a huge commercial success.

Turner is not the only star to rebound in the 1980s. Perhaps the most clear-cut example of the commercial power of baby-boomer nostalgia for the stars of the 1960s is the comeback of the Monkees. A group of questionable musical talent who disbanded in 1969, the Monkees returned to the top charts in 1986 with *Then and Now: The Best of the Monkees*. Their hit single, "That Was Then, This is Now" captured the sentiment of their return. Three members of the quartet set out on a sell-out concert tour, stimulated in part by re-runs on MTV of the old Monkees television show.

Unlike the Monkees, some stars from the 1960s have managed to sustain their popularity fairly consistently throughout the past two decades. Among these are Paul McCartney and Paul Simon. Simon's 1987 hit album, *Graceland*, is considered by some to be his best. Other stars from the 1960s returned to charts in the mid-eighties after long dry spells in the 1970s. Numbered among these artists are Aretha Franklin ("Jumpin' Jack Flash," 1986), John Fogerty (*Centerfield*, 1985) and Bob Dylan (*Biograph*, 1986).

Above: *Run-DMC at Madison Square Garden in New York in 1986.*
Left: *Tina Turner, the woman who taught Mick Jagger to dance, launched a successful solo career in 1985.*

Forty-five stars chime in on the chorus of
"We Are the World."

A new group that echoes the social commitment of the 1960s rock musicians took the charts by storm in 1987 with their fifth album, *The Joshua Tree*. U2 is an Irish quartet whose songs about racism, imperialism in Central America and spiritual growth remind many listeners of the idealistic songs of the 1960s. Their lead singer is Bono Vox (Paul Hewson); he is backed up on bass guitar by Adam Clayton, on drums by Larry Mullen, Jr., and on lead guitar by the Edge (a.k.a. David Evans). Their first relatively successful album, *War*, was released in 1983. Its most popular single, "Sunday Bloody Sunday" condemned the violence in Northern Ireland.

U2, like other rock musicians of the 1980s, often performs on behalf of social causes. Rock concerts as benefits hit the big time in 1985 with the coming together of a group of artists who called themselves USA for Africa (United Support of Artists for Africa). Their song, "We Are the World," raised millions of dollars to help the starving people of Ethiopia. Forty-five rock, pop, and country artists from the top of the national charts gathered together for the recording session. There were twenty-one soloists on the final recording of "We Are the World," a song written by Michael Jackson and Lionel Richie. The portrait of the musicians on the cover of the USA for Africa album presented a vivid picture of thirty years of rock and roll history. From Ray Charles, Stevie Wonder, and Tina Turner, representing the early years when rock developed from black rhythm and blues, to Cyndi Lauper, Bruce Springsteen, and Michael Jackson, nearly every important phase of rock history was there. Motown stars like Smokey Robinson and Diana Ross joined country rock stars like Kenny Rogers and Willie Nelson.

The success of USA for Africa inspired a number of other concerts to aid social causes. In 1985 Live Aid, a trans-Atlantic telethon of simultaneous concerts in Philadelphia and London, earned some $70 million for famine relief. The *New York Times* estimated that through television the size of the audience reached 1.5 billion. The performers included Paul McCartney, Tina Turner, the Who, Bob Dylan, Black Sabbath, and Crosby, Stills, Nash, and Young. In 1986 a six-city concert called Conspiracy of Hope raised three million dollars for Amnesty International and was credited with freeing South African trade-union leader Thozamile Gqweta. Other concerts were sponsored by Artists United Against Apartheid. Still other performers

*Tina Turner and Mick Jagger
performing at Live-Aid*

raised money for the victims of Chernobyl. In the summer of 1987, in an ironic twist on the 1960s, Crosby, Stills, and Nash, John Fogerty, Linda Ronstadt, James Brown and others performed in a July 4th concert to raise money for Vietnam veterans.

Concerts such as these represent the best of rock and roll. The power of this music, which has moved from roadhouses to Carnegie Hall, lies in its demand for attention, its challenge to ideas and conventions, its ability to highlight society's problems, and, through mass participation, to solve them. Noisy, gaudy, excessive, occasionally shocking, always changing, rock and roll music has a proud and colorful history.

INDEX

STACKS